Insight Secrets Collection

I0427552

Mindful **Money** Mastery

Navigating the Psychology of Finance in Your 20s

Comprehensive Guide to Building Financial Wellness, Overcoming Behavioral Hurdles, and Cultivating a Prosperous Future.

By Marc Scribnock

Table of Contents

2

Preface

Greetings and welcome to "Mindful Money Mastery: Navigating the Psychology of Finance in Your 20s." This book guides young people as they begin their path toward financial self-discovery and empowerment during a crucial phase of life. During your twenties, a period characterized by exploration, personal development, and pursuing aspirations, your financial connection becomes more important. This book endeavors to navigate you through the complex terrain of personal finance, providing valuable perspectives, tactics, and conscientious methods to cultivate financial wellness.

The concept of "Mindful Money Mastery" is based on the conviction that achieving financial empowerment extends beyond conventional ideas of budgeting and investing. It involves a more profound comprehension of the psychological variables that impact your financial choices. In the following pages, we will examine the complex relationship between your thoughts, emotions, and behaviors around money. We will provide techniques to develop awareness and purposefulness in your financial endeavors.

You can establish the foundation for a financially secure and satisfying future during your twenties. This book delves beyond the mere accumulation of money, focusing instead on harmonizing your financial choices with your core beliefs, goals, and desires. Every chapter is meticulously designed to tackle the precise obstacles and possibilities that emerge throughout this epochal decade, providing practical advice, tangible illustrations, and implementable measures.

As you go through the following chapters, see this book as a reliable guide that offers valuable perspectives to help you manage the intricacies of financial decision-making with attentiveness and intention. "Mindful Money Mastery" is specifically created to provide support and empowerment for those who are establishing financial goals, dealing with debt, making investments for the future, or considering their professional path.

Please be aware that this approach does not apply universally to all situations. The ideas presented in this book are intended to be customized to your specific circumstances since your financial path is unique and unparalleled. Approach each chapter with a receptive mindset and a readiness to delve into the profound facets of your financial relationship.

This book catalyzes inspiration, direction, and empowerment as you pursue financial expertise throughout your twenties. Cheers to conscientious financial planning, deliberate decision-making, and achieving monetary aspirations.

Chapter 1

Mindful Money Mastery

To achieve financial well-being, one must deeply comprehend financial concepts and the complex relationship between our thoughts and money. Introducing the first chapter of "Mindful Money Mastery: Understanding the Psychological Aspects of Finance in Your 20s." Within these pages, we will explore the fascinating intersection of behavioral psychology and personal finance, revealing the hidden truths underlying our choices about our finances. Understanding the psychological factors that influence financial habits is becoming more important for persons between 18 and 30 as they traverse the critical years of maturity. This book seeks to empower young people by unraveling the intricate web of ideas, emotions, and prejudices associated with financial problems. Its goal is to enable them to make educated and thoughtful decisions that will lead to a bright financial future.

"Introduction to the significance of comprehending the psychological aspects of finance."

Gaining a deep comprehension of the psychological aspects of money is crucial for effectively traversing the complex terrain of one's financial health. Personal finance encompasses more than just numerical calculations and following budgetary rules; it is closely interconnected with our emotions, beliefs, and behavioral tendencies. The importance of understanding the psychological foundations of financial decisions is evident since these elements significantly influence our monetary choices. This comprehension is a fundamental basis for people aiming to synchronize their financial actions with their long-term objectives, promoting a comprehensive strategy beyond the conventional budgeting and saving domains.

An essential component of studying the psychology of finance is acknowledging the distinct money mentality that influences our financial perspective. Our attitudes about money are deeply rooted and substantially affect our financial choices, stemming from childhood experiences and cultural factors. By examining the origins of these mindsets, people may understand the underlying causes of their financial habits, establishing the basis for a more aware and deliberate approach to money concerns.

Furthermore, comprehending the psychology of money empowers people to negotiate the emotional factors that often accompany financial choices. Emotions significantly influence our financial actions, ranging from the excitement of completing a purchase to the apprehension of debt. By promoting awareness of these emotional stimuli, people may devise tactics to control urges, make well-informed choices, and nurture a more healthful relationship with money.

Moreover, it is essential to acknowledge the significance of behavioral biases in influencing financial decision-making. Widespread cognitive traps, such as the need to avoid losses, the inclination to seek out information that confirms preexisting beliefs, and excessive self-assurance, may divert people off their intended path and impede their progress toward financial objectives. Gaining insight into these biases equips individuals with the necessary means to surmount them, cultivating a more logical and well-informed approach to making financial decisions.

To summarize, studying the psychology of finance involves more than just understanding the mind; it is a process of personal growth that leads to a deep understanding and control of one's financial decisions. By comprehending the complexities of our financial thinking, managing emotional effects, and acknowledging behavioral biases, people acquire the information and resources necessary to make deliberate, well-informed choices that align with their beliefs and goals. This thorough comprehension acts as a guiding principle, directing people toward financial success and satisfaction in a manner that surpasses conventional financial guidance.

Psychological variables have a significant impact on financial decisions. These factors include many cognitive and emotional processes that shape individuals' choices about money management, investment strategies, and risk tolerance. By understanding the psychological underpinnings of financial decision-making, one may get insights into the biases, heuristics, and irrational behaviors that often lead to suboptimal financial outcomes.

Psychological considerations significantly impact our financial decisions, influencing the complex fabric of our economic habits and choices. A critical psychological determinant is our money mentality, which encompasses a set of ideas and attitudes toward money that often originate from early experiences and cultural influences. These attitudes influence our views on money, success, and financial stability, eventually shaping our choices about expenditure, savings, and investments. Gaining a deep understanding of the origins of our attitudes and beliefs about money is essential for making informed decisions about our finances. This understanding allows us to uncover the underlying motives and biases influencing our economic activities.

Emotions are pivotal in the decision-making process, substantially impacting financial decisions. The pleasure obtained from a purchase or the anxiety linked to debt might result in impulsive choices that may not correspond with our overarching financial objectives. Acknowledging and handling these emotional impacts is crucial for a well-rounded and purposeful approach to financial affairs. Moreover, the apprehension of losing something often surpasses the possibility of gaining, referred to as loss aversion. This aversion might cause people to abstain from essential risks or adhere to unproductive financial practices, impeding their overall financial well-being.

Behavioral biases, which arise from cognitive shortcuts and heuristics, also affect the psychological aspect of making financial decisions. Confirmation bias, for example, motivates people to actively search for information that aligns with their previous ideas, which may result in selective attention and faulty decision-making. To overcome these biases, one must possess a heightened awareness of their presence and a dedication to making judgments based on objective data rather than misleading perceptions.

Social and cultural forces further contribute to the psychological variables that shape financial choices.

Influence from peers, social norms, and cultural expectations may affect how individuals spend money, make lifestyle choices, and even choose their careers. It is crucial for people who want to match their financial decisions with their personal beliefs and ambitions to acknowledge these external effects. This will help them adopt a more deliberate approach to their economic actions.

To summarize, the interaction of psychological elements in financial decision-making is complex and diverse. By comprehending and tackling our attitudes towards money, managing emotional factors, acknowledging behavioral prejudices, and considering social and cultural impacts, folks may acquire enhanced authority over their financial futures. This knowledge establishes the basis for a deliberate and attentive approach to financial concerns, enabling people to make well-informed choices that result in financial prosperity and satisfaction.

It is establishing the foundation for achieving financial prosperity. Preparing for financial well-being requires establishing a solid base that includes comprehending, recognizing, and purposefully planning. To embark on this transforming path, it is crucial to acknowledge the subtle correlation between psychology and money. Recognizing that personal finance encompasses more than simply numerical figures. It includes an intricate interaction of emotions, ideas, and actions that greatly influence financial outcomes. By adopting this comprehensive viewpoint, people are ready to begin a voyage that surpasses conventional financial guidance, delving into the intricacies of their financial psyche.

Furthermore, the path requires investigating the roots of one's financial thinking. Childhood experiences and cultural influences are essential in shaping individual ideas around money. Unraveling these strands yields a deep comprehension of the origins of financial practices. It establishes the foundation for a more mindful and deliberate approach to financial concerns, enabling people to harmonize their monetary choices with their principles and goals.

Recognizing the current components of personal finance is another crucial factor in establishing a foundation for financial prosperity. Young people today have both possibilities and problems in a time characterized by unparalleled access to knowledge and financial resources. The emergence of the gig economy, shifting job paths, and a dynamic economic environment all contribute to a distinct financial journey for this particular cohort. Acknowledging and tackling these modern elements guarantees that the path toward financial prosperity remains relevant and adaptable to the present circumstances people encounter.

Moreover, the process of setting the scene entails the introduction of a guiding principle that will direct the voyage. The notion of "Mindful Money Mastery" arises as a fundamental concept, promoting a comprehensive strategy that integrates mindfulness into financial decisions. In this context, mindfulness is being completely present and conscious of one's thoughts, emotions, and actions about finances. This fundamental concept emphasizes the significance of achieving financial success and establishing a profound connection between one's beliefs, objectives, and financial choices.

Preparing for the path to financial stability is a thorough procedure that includes acknowledging the psychological elements of finance, investigating the roots of one's money attitude, confronting current financial circumstances, and adopting a guiding philosophy. As people begin this transforming journey, they possess the knowledge and deliberate mindset required to negotiate the intricacies of personal finance, leading to financial prosperity and a more meaningful and purposeful connection with money.

Chapter 2

Money Mindset

We start on our financial adventure by delving into the realm of cognition. Chapter 2, titled "Money Mindset," examines the ideas and attitudes influencing our connection with money. This chapter establishes the groundwork for a significant change in our perception and interaction with our finances by dispelling ingrained misconceptions about money and promoting a positive and empowered attitude towards it.

" Investigating personal attitudes and ideas on money."

Examining individual attitudes and ideas toward money is essential to understanding the complex connection between psychology and personal finance. Individuals' attitudes towards money often act as a perspective through which they see their financial situations and make choices. These attitudes are ingrained in individual pasts, covering childhood events, cultural influences, and societal norms. By exploring these particular attitudes, people understand the cognitive structures that influence their financial habits, facilitating a more deliberate and aware approach to money management.

Acknowledging the range of emotions associated with money is an essential factor in examining individual attitudes. The emotional terrain around money encompasses many sentiments, including a sense of security, achievement, fear, and guilt. These emotions are very individual and subjective. By recognizing and accepting these feelings, people may effectively manage their financial choices with enhanced self-awareness, cultivating a more sound and equitable connection with money.

Furthermore, personal beliefs and opinions around finances can become evident via distinct actions and recurring trends. Certain people may exhibit a propensity for saving, placing a high value on financial stability and long-term objectives, while others may tend to favor spending, pursuing instant satisfaction. Studying these behavioral inclinations offers a valuable understanding of the practical consequences of one's attitude toward money and allows for deliberate modifications that align with personal financial objectives.

Cultural and socioeconomic factors significantly influence individual opinions regarding money. External influences, such as cultural norms and social expectations, shape ideas that impact financial decision-making. By acknowledging the effects of these pressures, people may differentiate between external expectations and their financial objectives, thus promoting a more empowered and genuine approach to managing money.

Examining personal attitudes and ideas around money is essential in achieving conscious control over finances. By identifying the subtle emotional aspects, comprehending behavioral patterns, and appreciating the effect of culture and society, people acquire the necessary skills to navigate their financial choices with purpose and deliberation. This investigation is a potent catalyst for harmonizing one's financial actions with personal beliefs and objectives, cultivating a more intentional and satisfying connection with money.

"Identifying and debunking money-related fallacies and misunderstandings."

Recognizing and questioning false beliefs and misunderstandings about money is vital to promoting a sound and knowledgeable attitude to managing one's finances. We encounter many ideas and cultural stories around money, some of which may not correspond with financial circumstances. Through actively recognizing and questioning these misconceptions, people may free themselves from unproductive thought habits, enabling them to make more knowledgeable and deliberate financial choices.

A common misconception often focuses on the notion that increased wealth directly correlates with heightened levels of pleasure. Although financial security is undeniably crucial, research regularly demonstrates that there is a declining relationship between money and happiness above a certain level. Questioning this misconception enables people to focus on elements of life beyond monetary riches, cultivating a more comprehensive outlook on overall well-being.

Another prevalent fallacy is the notion that debt is always negative. Although high-interest debt might be unpleasant, it is crucial to recognize that not all debt is the same. Mortgages and school debts, for instance, might be seen as investments in prospective potential. By comprehending the intricacies of various forms of debt, people may make well-informed judgments on the timing and manner in which they appropriately use credit.

The prevailing misconception that investment is only reserved for the affluent is unfounded. It is crucial to challenge this notion, particularly for younger folks. Individuals may use various investment platforms and tactics to begin investments with even small amounts. Dispelling this misconception empowers individuals to use the potential of exponential development and accumulate wealth gradually.

Furthermore, it is essential to dispel the misunderstanding that financial literacy is exclusive to professionals or those in the finance business. Financial literacy is a vital life skill that enables people to make well-informed choices about budgeting, investing, and general money management. Disputing this misconception highlights the significance of knowledge and self-empowerment in effectively managing the intricacies of personal finance.

To summarize, recognizing and questioning false beliefs and misunderstandings about money is crucial in attaining a state of conscious control and expertise in managing finances. By challenging widely accepted assumptions, people can approach their financial choices lucidly and purposefully. This method cultivates a firmly rooted mentality, allowing people to construct a more robust and meaningful financial future.

"Presenting cultivating a positive and balanced attitude towards finances."

Introducing the notion of a healthy money attitude is like establishing the foundation for a transforming journey toward mastering money with mindfulness. A healthy money mentality encompasses more than just numerical figures or financial tactics; it adopts a comprehensive perspective that acknowledges the deep interrelation between an individual's ideas, emotions, and actions around money. A healthy money attitude is fundamentally based on self-awareness and intentionality, encouraging people to connect positively with their financial well-being.

An essential aspect of cultivating a positive attitude towards money is recognizing that it serves to achieve one's desired lifestyle rather than cause worry or unease. It entails cultivating a mentality that perceives financial choices not as limiting restrictions but as chances to harmonize one's activities with individual values and long-term objectives. By adopting this viewpoint, people may transition from a scarcity mentality to one of plenty, seeing the possibilities for progress, satisfaction, and meaning in their financial path.

Furthermore, a sound financial mentality highlights the need for self-compassion and resilience when facing monetary difficulties. The program acknowledges that obstacles are an inherent aspect of any financial endeavor and promotes a mindset of inquiry rather than criticism when facing them. Nurturing resilience empowers people to recover from failures, derive lessons from experiences, and adjust their financial plans to foster enduring welfare.

A healthy money attitude involves changing from relying on external standards and social expectations. Individuals with a healthy money attitude prioritize their own beliefs and objectives instead of comparing themselves to others or conforming to cultural conventions. This transformation enables people to make financial decisions that are more genuine and purposeful, giving them the ability to choose a path that aligns with their own goals of success and pleasure.

To summarize, introducing a healthy money mentality signifies the start of a revolutionary path toward conscientious and intentional financial management. Through developing self-awareness, accepting wealth, creating resilience, and prioritizing personal values above external expectations, people may establish the foundation for a healthy and empowered connection with money. This change in perspective serves as both the driving force behind achieving financial prosperity and as a fundamental building block for a more satisfying and purposeful existence.

Chapter 3

Goal Setting and Financial Planning

Chapter 3 focuses on the practical elements of financial empowerment, namely goal setting and financial planning. Discover the potential of establishing SMART financial objectives and get the necessary techniques for developing a budget and constructing a thorough financial blueprint that corresponds with your ambitions.

"The significance of establishing objectives in achieving financial prosperity."

Goal setting is crucial in achieving financial success as it provides people with a clear plan to manage the intricacies of personal finance. Establishing explicit and attainable financial objectives is a potent catalyst, imbuing one's financial expedition with profound determination and guidance. Setting clear goals, such as saving for a housing down payment, financing college, or establishing an emergency fund, offers a concrete structure for making decisions and allocating resources.

Furthermore, financial objectives function as a standard for evaluating advancement and achievement. Lacking explicit goals, people may need help in assessing their progress or determining the need to modify their financial plans. Establishing milestones enables regular assessments, commemorating accomplishments, and readjusting objectives as conditions change. This iterative procedure guarantees that people maintain their focus on their financial ambitions and offers a chance for ongoing development and improvement.

Goal setting is crucial for developing financial discipline and fostering responsible conduct. Setting immediate and future objectives motivates people to make purposeful decisions that align with their aims. This may include financial planning, restraining superfluous expenditures, or embracing frugal behaviors. The dedication to attaining precise financial goals promotes a feeling of responsibility, establishing the foundation for behaviors that lead to long-term financial prosperity.

Furthermore, financial objectives contribute to a feeling of financial stability and tranquility. Financial objectives, such as establishing an emergency fund for unforeseen needs or preparing for retirement to guarantee enduring financial security, play a crucial role in fostering comprehensive financial wellness. By adopting this proactive strategy, people may confront the future with assurance since they have implemented tangible measures to achieve their financial goals.

To summarize, goal setting has a multifaceted function in achieving financial success, acting as a guiding principle, a means of measurement, a tool for enhancing discipline, and a source of financial stability. Through establishing and pursuing well-defined financial objectives, people equip themselves with the ability to make knowledgeable choices, foster favorable financial behaviors, and eventually attain a level of financial prosperity that is in harmony with their ambitions and principles.

"Establish specific, measurable, achievable, relevant, and time-bound financial objectives for the immediate and distant future."

Developing SMART financial objectives is an organized and efficient way to achieve immediate and long-term financial ambitions. The SMART framework, Specific, Measurable, Achievable, Relevant, and Time-bound, offers a systematic approach to goal formulation that improves clarity, responsibility, and achievement.

SMART financial objectives are characterized by their specificity, indicating that they are well-defined and explicitly articulate the desired achievements. Instead of an ambiguous objective such as "save money," a precise objective may be "accumulate $5,000 for an emergency fund within the upcoming 12 months."

This level of precision offers a distinct objective, minimizing potential confusion and enhancing the probability of doing the task well.

Measurable objectives allow people to monitor their progress and ascertain whether they have effectively accomplished their target. Utilizing quantifiable indicators, such as precise monetary values or proportions, enables a concrete evaluation of the proximity to achieving the objective. An example of a measurable objective may be "decrease monthly non-essential expenses by 15%."

Attainable objectives are practical and viable, considering the person's financial circumstances and limitations. Although ambition is praiseworthy, establishing goals that are too ambitious might result in feelings of dissatisfaction and loss of drive. A feasible aim is by an individual's financial capability and permits consistent and enduring advancement.

Significant aims are purposeful and in harmony with an individual's overarching financial goals. They must be closely linked to an individual's comprehensive financial strategy and contribute to achieving financial prosperity. Every objective should have a distinct role in propelling one's financial progress, whether accumulating funds for a particular acquisition or allocating resources for long-term expansion. Ultimately, time-bound objectives are accompanied by a fixed timeframe, instilling a feeling of immediacy and dedication. Introducing a specific time range allows organizations to create goals, avoid the tendency to delay, and encourage a steady and persistent effort. An example of a goal with a specific time frame is to "eliminate a $10,000 credit card debt within the upcoming 18 months."

To summarize, establishing SMART financial objectives guarantees a systematic and strategic method for financial planning. By formulating precise, quantifiable, attainable, pertinent, and time-limited objectives, people empower themselves to effectively manage immediate benchmarks and long-term financial ambitions with clarity, concentration, and an increased likelihood of accomplishment.

"Fundamentals of budgeting and financial planning."

Proficiency in budgeting and financial planning is a crucial cornerstone for enduring financial prosperity. Budgeting is a proactive and strategic instrument enabling people to gain authority over their money, align their spending with priorities, and strive toward their financial objectives. Financial planning encompasses more than just budgeting and entails a holistic approach to managing income, spending, savings, and investments in the short and long term.

The budgeting process starts with comprehensively comprehending one's income and expenditures. Determining the sources of income, whether derived from a regular wage, supplementary business venture, or financial investments, offers a comprehensive understanding of the available financial assets. Concurrently, organizing and monitoring expenditures, including essential expenses such as rent and utilities and optional spending on leisure activities like meals, enables consumers to evaluate the destination of their funds and pinpoint prospective areas for modification.

Developing a budget entails establishing expenditure boundaries for each category, considering revenue and financial objectives. This allocation guarantees that people prioritize necessary needs while simultaneously setting aside cash for savings and discretionary spending. Users may shorten the process using budgeting tools, applications, or conventional spreadsheets to gain immediate access to financial activities and maintain their financial goals.

Financial planning is a comprehensive approach that combines budgeting with long-term objectives, such as purchasing a house, saving for college, or preparing for retirement. The process entails evaluating an individual's financial well-being, including total assets, liabilities, and funds set aside for unforeseen circumstances. Financial planning enables people to devise tactics for minimizing debt, establishing a contingency fund, and carefully allocating investments to foster future growth.

Consistently evaluating and modifying the budget and financial plan is essential to reflect changes in personal circumstances, economic volatility, and growing objectives. Versatility and adjustability are crucial elements of effective financial planning. Periodic reviews provide a chance to commemorate financial achievements, reevaluate goals, and adjust plans to match changing conditions.

To summarize, acquiring proficiency in budgeting and financial planning fundamentals is a pivotal stride toward achieving financial prosperity. By adopting budgeting as a means of daily financial management and incorporating it into a holistic financial strategy, people may travel their financial path with purpose, make well-informed choices, and strive for a future of financial stability and success.

Chapter 4

Emotional Influences on Spending

Explore the intricate relationship between emotions and spending patterns in Chapter 4. We analyze the psychological stimuli that result in impulsive expenditure, offering practical techniques to foster awareness and purposefulness in your monetary choices.

"Comprehending the emotional stimuli that prompt individuals to engage in spending."

Gaining insight into the emotional stimuli that prompt spending is vital in cultivating a conscientious and deliberate approach to managing one's finances. Emotions significantly influence our financial habits, often influencing spending choices that may not align with our long-term objectives. By exploring the emotional dimensions of expenditure, people may understand their patterns, make more deliberate decisions, and cultivate a more healthful relationship with finances.

Stress is a frequently encountered emotional stimulus that may lead to expenditure. During times of stress, people may turn to retail therapy or make lavish purchases to seek comfort or temporary relief. By acknowledging this emotional connection, people can investigate alternate methods of managing stress that does not need spending, such as participating in physical activity, practicing meditation, or pursuing hobbies.

Another psychological stimulus is the want for immediate satisfaction. In a society where internet shopping provides convenient and expedited access, the temptation to make impulsive purchases and get them promptly might be vital. Recognizing the importance of instant gratification, people might intentionally stop before making purchases to assess whether the expenditure corresponds with their overall financial objectives.

Social effects may act as emotional stimuli for spending, particularly in the era of social media when the need to conform to trends and project a particular lifestyle is widespread. By acknowledging the power of social comparison and peer influence, people may cultivate an enhanced consciousness of their spending motivations, enabling them to make choices that align with their ideals rather than external pressures.

Spending may also be influenced by emotional triggers associated with self-esteem and identity.

Acquisitions can enhance self-worth or reflect a particular image to others. Gaining a more profound comprehension of these emotional connections enables people to investigate other paths for constructing self-esteem and identity that are not dependent on material items.

Finally, the apprehension of being excluded (FOMO) is a powerful emotional stimulus that may stimulate expenditure. Events of a social nature, travel encounters, or time-limited bargains might induce a feeling of urgency, prompting consumers to engage in impulsive buying. By acknowledging FOMO as a stimulus, people may evaluate whether their spending aligns with their priorities and whether the worry is warranted.

To summarize, comprehending the emotional stimuli that lead to expenditure is essential in developing financial awareness. By understanding the impact of stress on spending habits, the need for immediate satisfaction, the influence of society, the connection between self-esteem and spending, and the fear of missing out, people may make deliberate decisions that are in line with their own beliefs, priorities, and long-term financial objectives. This heightened awareness shifts spending from a passive reaction to an empowered and deliberate decision-making process.

"Methods for controlling impulsive purchasing and emotional expenditure."

To effectively manage impulsive purchasing and emotional spending, it is necessary to use tactics that encourage mindfulness, self-awareness, and deliberate decision-making. The next stage is to identify the stimuli that prompt impulsive expenditures, followed by employing pragmatic strategies to restrain these behaviors and cultivate more sound financial habits.

A practical approach is implementing a "cooling-off" time. Consumers might implement a delay period before purchasing, particularly for discretionary products, whether a day, a week or an extended duration. This momentary break provides an opportunity for contemplation, allowing consumers to evaluate whether their need to purchase is a passing whim or a legitimate necessity. It incorporates a purposeful measure into the decision-making process, restraining the impulsiveness of spending driven by emotions.

Formulating a financial plan and adhering to it is an additional productive tactic. Setting specific spending limitations for different categories and following these restrictions offers a well-organized framework for making financial choices. Individuals can designate

33

particular amounts of money for discretionary spending, enabling them to experience satisfaction without compromising their long-term financial objectives. This approach promotes deliberate expenditure within predetermined boundaries, reducing the likelihood of impulsive acquisitions.

Using physical currency instead of electronic payment methods is a concrete approach to controlling impulsive expenditures driven by emotions. The tangible transfer of currency elicits a more immediate effect on our consciousness of expenditure. When people choose to use physical currency for non-essential transactions, they can directly see the money physically leave their possession, strengthening the link between spending and its monetary repercussions. This increased consciousness may serve as an inherent barrier to spontaneous acquisitions.

Meticulously monitoring expenditures and analyzing spending trends is crucial for effectively curbing impulsive spending. Utilizing tools such as budgeting applications or financial software may provide a comprehensive analysis of the allocation of funds. Through regular analysis of their expenditure patterns, people may detect patterns, identify possible areas of excessive spending, and make educated modifications to match their actions with their financial objectives.

Participating in emotionally fulfilling activities that do not need expenditure is a proactive approach.

Engaging in hobbies, dedicating time to loved ones, or embarking on personal growth pursuits are alternatives to shop therapy. By channeling emotional demands into gratifying and non-financial pursuits, people may disrupt the pattern of emotional consumption and cultivate a more harmonized and enduring attitude to their whole state of being.

To summarize, practical approaches to controlling impulsive purchasing and emotional expenditure include mindfulness, strategic planning, and deliberate decision-making. Using strategies such as implementing waiting periods, establishing and following budgets, utilizing cash transactions, monitoring expenditures, and seeking alternate emotional satisfaction, people may empower themselves to make deliberate and well-informed decisions that align with their overall financial goals. These tactics restrain impulsive spending and foster a more conscious and intentional attitude to personal finance.

"We are cultivating a deliberate and mindful attitude to spending."

Adopting a deliberate and purposeful attitude to spending is a profound process that fosters mindfulness, self-awareness, and a profound comprehension of one's financial preferences. Essentially, this strategy promotes a shift from impulsive spending behaviors to a more intentional and reflective approach to managing one's financial resources.

To begin a deliberate strategy, it is essential to define unambiguous financial objectives. These objectives act as a beacon, offering a structure for every expense. By aligning spending with particular goals, such as saving for an emergency fund, a dream trip, or long-term investments, individuals may guarantee that every financial choice they make adds to their overall plan.

Practicing mindful budgeting is a fundamental aspect of intentional expenditure. Creating a budget includes classifying expenses, strategically allocating monies, and monitoring progress. By comprehending the allocation of funds and allocating precise amounts to distinct categories, people get clarity and authority over their financial decisions. By adopting this deliberate strategy, individuals can make well-informed choices and avoid unneeded or impulsive spending.

Cultivating thankfulness and contentment is essential to adopting a mindful approach to spending. Recognizing and valuing one's current possessions and circumstances cultivates a mentality of contentment, diminishing the inclination towards excessive purchasing motivated by social pressures or comparisons with others. This change in viewpoint enables folks to shift their attention away from accumulating material stuff and towards cherishing life events and significant connections.

Regularly evaluating expenditure priorities is crucial for keeping a mindful and deliberate attitude. Ensuring expenses align with current objectives as circumstances change and goals develop is essential. The continuous assessment avoids the tendency to engage in thoughtless spending habits and motivates people to adjust their financial choices according to life's ever-changing circumstances.

Finally, developing awareness in everyday financial operations enhances a deliberate approach. This entails maintaining attentiveness and complete consciousness throughout financial activities, whether purchasing or examining a bank statement. By actively participating in financial decision-making, people may identify and address possible risks, evaluate the compatibility of expenses with objectives, and consistently improve their strategies to enhance their financial welfare.

To summarize, cultivating a deliberate and thoughtful attitude to spending is a comprehensive endeavor that encompasses goal establishment, conscientious budgeting, appreciation, periodic evaluation, and general attentiveness in financial endeavors. By embracing this methodology, people may revolutionize their connection with money, guaranteeing that every spending aligns with their beliefs, objectives, and financial goals. Adopting this intentional approach enhances financial prosperity and cultivates a more satisfying and meaningful existence.

Chapter 5

Fundamentals of Investment

Chapter 5 elucidates the realm of investing by presenting essential ideas such as risk tolerance, diversification, and the phenomenon of compounding. Acquire the necessary information to begin your financial adventure confidently.

"The first point is an overview of the basic investment principles."

Understanding the basic investing principles is the starting point for accumulating money and ensuring long-term financial stability. Investing is allocating funds with the anticipation of earning long-term returns, and comprehending the fundamentals is crucial for making well-informed and planned financial choices.

Investing fundamentally involves using capital to achieve further financial returns. The stock market is a crucial avenue for investment, allowing people to buy shares in firms that are publicly traded. Stocks symbolize equity in a corporation, and their worth might oscillate according to diverse aspects, such as the corporation's performance, market circumstances, and economic patterns.

Diversification is a critical tenet in the field of investing. Diversification is allocating assets among asset classes, sectors, and geographic locations to mitigate risk. Portfolio diversification mitigates the adverse effects of underperforming investments by capitalizing on the favorable performance of alternative assets. This method is an essential element in managing risk while seeking possible gains.

The interdependence between risk and return characterizes investing. Typically, investments that provide more potential for profit also include greater degrees of risk. It is essential to comprehend one's risk tolerance, which refers to the capacity to endure changes in investment worth. The method of balancing risk and return is tailored to each individual's financial objectives, time frame, and tolerance for market fluctuations.

Time is crucial in determining the level of success in investing. Compounding is a powerful mechanism that enables assets to increase in value over time as the profits generated from the initial investment are reinvested, creating more profits. Commencing investment early and maintaining dedication to a long-term plan may enhance the impact of compounding, offering the possibility of substantial wealth accumulation.

Finally, maintaining awareness and acquiring knowledge is an ongoing component of successful investment. Markets transform, economic circumstances change, and fresh investment prospects arise. Staying updated on financial news, market trends, and investment techniques enable people to make well-informed judgments, adjust to changing circumstances, and negotiate the intricacies of the investing environment.

Ultimately, the first exposition on the core principles of investment establishes the foundation for people to begin a path toward financial expansion and acquiring wealth. Understanding the stock market, adopting diversification, managing risk and return, acknowledging the influence of time, and being well-informed are fundamental principles in establishing a solid basis for prosperous investment. Acquiring this information enables people to make well-informed choices and strive towards accomplishing their financial objectives.

"Assessment of one's willingness to accept and handle potential risks."

Risk tolerance and risk management are essential components of the investing process, serving a vital function in assisting people in navigating the intricacies of financial markets and making well-informed choices that match their financial objectives and comfort thresholds.

Risk tolerance pertains to an individual's capacity and inclination to withstand variations in the value of their assets. It is an inherently subjective trait shaped by variables such as monetary objectives, duration of investment, and psychological fortitude. Evaluating risk tolerance is essential in creating an investing portfolio corresponding to an individual's comfort and goals. Gaining insight into an individual's risk tolerance enables them to find a middle ground between the possibility of greater profits and the instability associated with more precarious ventures.

Risk management is executing methods to mitigate the consequences of unfavorable market fluctuations on an investment portfolio. Diversification is a crucial risk management strategy that distributes assets across various asset classes, sectors, and geographic areas. Diversification mitigates the adverse effects of underperformance in a specific investment by avoiding over-reliance on a single investment. This strategy provides a seamless and secure path toward achieving financial objectives.

An additional crucial aspect of risk management is establishing explicit investing goals and harmonizing them with a well-defined financial strategy. By setting attainable objectives and a specific timeframe, one may develop an investing plan that aligns with one's risk tolerance. Consistently evaluating and modifying the investment portfolio in response to alterations in financial circumstances or market conditions is essential for proficient risk management.

A thorough understanding of the many risk categories is crucial when formulating a complete risk management plan. Investors may encounter several risks, such as market, interest rate, and credit risks. By acknowledging these potential hazards, people may make well-informed choices, apply appropriate risk mitigation strategies, and effectively negotiate the constantly evolving terrain of financial markets.

To summarize, risk tolerance and risk management are fundamental principles for achieving investment success. Evaluating and comprehending an individual's capacity for accepting risk, spreading investments over different assets, harmonizing tactics with financial objectives, and acknowledging the many forms of risks all contribute to a comprehensive strategy for handling the uncertainties inherent in financial markets. By embracing these ideas, investors may construct robust portfolios that endure throughout time and enhance the probability of attaining long-term financial prosperity.

"The benefits of diversification and the exponential growth potential of compounding."

Diversification and compounding are two essential factors that greatly enhance the performance of an investing portfolio. Collectively, they provide a potent approach for amassing wealth, mitigating risk, and achieving enduring financial prosperity.

Diversification entails the allocation of assets among various asset classes, sectors, and geographic areas. The objective is to construct a diversified portfolio that does not excessively depend on the success of any one investment. Through diversification, investors can diminish the influence of underperforming assets on their entire investment portfolio. This has the potential to minimize risk and improve the consistency of returns. This technique recognizes the volatility of financial markets and seeks to mitigate the inherent risks by ensuring that the benefits from one investment offset the losses from another.

Compounding is a potent mechanism that magnifies the expansion of assets as time progresses. Compounding refers to the process where the profits created from an investment lead to more profits, resulting in a cumulative impact. The greater the duration of compounding, the more pronounced its effect becomes. Commencing investments early and having a prolonged outlook are essential elements for leveraging the benefits of compounding. The compounding impact is exponential, potentially enabling people to amass significant wealth even with little beginning contributions.

The combination of diversity and the compounding effect forms a robust approach for both accumulating and safeguarding wealth. Diversification mitigates the chance for losses while compounding amplifies the growth prospects of the portfolio. The harmonious interaction of these two concepts enhances the efficiency and durability of one's financial journey, equipping people with the resources to accomplish their long-term financial objectives.

Furthermore, combining diversity and compounding synergistically generates a well-rounded and enduring strategy for managing risk and maximizing returns. Diversification mitigates risk by distributing investments over many assets while compounding optimizes investment returns by enabling profits to expand exponentially. This combination facilitates the development of a comprehensive portfolio that aims to limit risk while maximizing the potential for long-term wealth accumulation.

Diversity and the compounding effect are essential strategies for achieving investment success. Through the strategic integration of risk management via diversity and the wealth accumulation potential of compounding, people may create robust portfolios that endure over time and strive towards attaining their financial goals. These concepts provide a solid basis for effectively navigating the ever-changing environment of financial markets and achieving the benefits of consistent, long-term investment.

Chapter 6

Behavioral Biases in Finance

Explore the complex network of cognitive biases that impact financial decisions in Chapter 6. Explore the nuanced ways our thoughts may misguide us and learn practical strategies to overcome these biases, guaranteeing.

"Investigating prevalent cognitive biases in the process of making financial decisions."

Studying prevalent cognitive biases in financial decision-making exposes how our brains might diverge from rationality in money matters. Cognitive biases refer to consistent patterns of divergence from standard or reasonable judgment, often resulting from mental shortcuts or emotional effects. It is essential for investors and anyone making financial choices to acknowledge these biases since they may substantially influence the results.

Loss aversion is a common cognitive bias in which people experience losses' negative impact more intensely than similar gains' positive effects. This bias might result in excessively cautious decision-making, as people may be more likely to prioritize avoiding losses rather than pursuing possible profits. Understanding and reducing loss aversion is crucial for establishing a well-balanced and logical investing strategy.

Overconfidence bias is a prevalent cognitive distortion characterized by people's inflated perception of their talents and expertise. Overconfidence in financial decision-making may result in frequent trading, unjustified risk-taking, and a lack of thorough evaluation of possible drawbacks. To address this prejudice, one must develop a genuine self-awareness and actively seek out various opinions to counteract excessive confidence.

Anchoring bias refers to the tendency of people to excessively depend on the first piece of information they come across while making choices. Within a financial framework, this is an excessive focus on the buying price of a stock or the first expenditure of an investment. One must consciously analyze and reassess knowledge in light of changing conditions or new facts to overcome anchoring bias.

The availability heuristic is a cognitive bias in which people make judgments based on easily accessible information, often from recent or noteworthy occurrences. This cognitive bias might result in excessive focus on current market patterns or economic events within financial decision-making. To counteract the availability heuristic, one must intentionally gather a more comprehensive array of knowledge and refrain from relying too heavily on readily available but possibly biased data.

Confirmation bias is the inclination to prefer information supporting pre-established views or attitudes. Within the financial domain, this cognitive bias might prompt investors to selectively construe information that aligns with their preexisting perspectives and disregard evidence that contradicts them. To mitigate confirmation bias, one must actively pursue a range of opinions, engage in comprehensive study, and maintain receptiveness to various ideas.

Examining prevalent cognitive biases in financial decision-making is essential as a fundamental measure in promoting more logical and well-informed choices. By acknowledging these biases, people can approach financial choices with enhanced self-awareness, decreasing the probability of succumbing to cognitive distortions that may weaken rational judgment and hinder long-term financial prosperity. Through proactive efforts to acknowledge and confront these biases, investors may enhance their ability to make impartial, calculated, and congruent judgments that match their overarching financial objectives.

"The influence of biases on investing decisions and their subsequent effect on financial results."

Biases significantly influence investment decisions and financial consequences, leading to decision-making processes that may diverge from logical and objective considerations. Comprehending the widespread existence of biases is essential for investors, as it may greatly influence portfolio management, risk tolerance, and overall financial prosperity.

Biases have a significant influence on financial decisions, mainly via the occurrence of overtrading, which is caused by the overconfidence bias. Investors with an inflated perception of their capacity to forecast market fluctuations may partake in excessive purchasing and selling, leading to increased transaction expenses and possibly compromising long-term gains. Excessive self-assurance may also result in insufficient diversification, as people may believe their selected investments surpass the overall market performance.

Loss aversion, a well-observed cognitive bias, may influence investing decisions since people tend to respond emotionally to declines in the market. Investors may exhibit excessive risk aversion and divest their assets during market downturns because they fear more losses. Motivated by the inclination to prevent losses rather than seek profits, this conduct may lead to lost chances for recovery when markets bounce back.

The anchoring bias affects investing choices by inducing people to concentrate on specific reference points, such as purchase pricing or past performance. Investors often rely on these reference points to shape their expectations and judgments, which may result in less-than-ideal choices and a hesitancy to adapt tactics as circumstances change. This prejudice might impede flexibility and restrict investors from making choices based on prevailing market circumstances.

Confirmation bias affects investment decisions by shaping how people search for and interpret information. Investors tend to choose information that aligns with their opinions and devalue evidence that contradicts their perspectives. This bias may result in a need for more diversity as people may disregard useful findings contrary to their preconceived assumptions, thereby limiting the effectiveness of their financial strategy.

Herding behavior, influenced by social factors and the fear of missing out (FOMO), is another way biases affect investing decisions. Investors may need to complete comprehensive research to avoid herd behavior, resulting in the formation of market bubbles and eventual collapses. Engaging in herding behavior may lead to the inflation of asset values and increased

51

market instability, which can negatively affect the financial results of individuals who give in to the influence of group mentality.

Ultimately, biases significantly impact investing decisions and notably affect financial results. Identifying these biases is vital to developing a systematic and logical approach to investment. To limit the influence of biases and make choices that line with their long-term financial goals, investors should cultivate self-awareness, use a variety of tactics, and actively seek out alternative opinions.

"Strategies to counteract and alleviate cognitive biases."

It is crucial to overcome and reduce cognitive biases to make rational financial choices and attain long-term investing success. Although biases are deeply rooted in human psychology, investors may use several ways to mitigate their influence and cultivate a more logical and unbiased decision-making process.

A very successful strategy involves developing self-awareness. Investors may mitigate the impact of cognitive biases by identifying their presence and taking measures to minimize their influence. Engaging in regular introspection and analyzing the cognitive processes that influenced prior judgments enables people to recognize persistent biases and devise practical approaches to mitigate them in future situations.

Expanding the variety of information sources is an effective strategy to mitigate confirmation bias. Proactively pursuing other opinions, actively participating in discussions with many ideas, and considering a wide array of information might assist investors in avoiding the pitfall of selectively interpreting evidence that aligns with their preconceived notions. This methodology promotes a thorough and equitable examination, mitigating the influence of confirmation bias on the process of making decisions.

Utilizing decision-making frameworks and checklists is an effective method to reduce different cognitive biases. Individuals may incorporate structure and discipline into decision-making by defining explicit criteria and predetermined methods for analyzing investment prospects. These frameworks serve as a roadmap, assisting investors in making more methodical and unbiased selections rather than giving in to impulsive or emotionally motivated choices.

Participating in collaborative decision-making and actively soliciting information from others is a very successful strategy for mitigating the adverse effects of overconfidence and groupthink biases. Constructive criticism and various viewpoints provide significant insights that may challenge personal biases and enhance decision-making by providing a more comprehensive perspective. Promoting an atmosphere that fosters open communication helps in reducing the likelihood of making judgments in isolation.

Finally, using decision-making norms and adhering to them is a strategy that effectively mitigates the impact of emotional biases. Creating pre-established benchmarks for purchasing or divesting assets, establishing precise limits for risk tolerance, and following these guidelines despite market volatility effectively inhibit impulsive and emotionally influenced choices. This method instills a degree of self-control that may supersede the emotional prejudices that often result in less-than-ideal financial results.

To summarize, strategies to address and reduce cognitive biases include self-awareness, diversity of information sources, decision-making frameworks, collaborative methods, and enforcing norms. Through the active use of these strategies, investors may improve their capacity to make logical, unbiased choices and effectively traverse the intricacies of financial markets, increasing their chances of achieving favorable outcomes.

Chapter 7

Debt Management

Chapter 7 delves into the practicalities of debt and reveals methods for prudent borrowing and efficient debt management. Acquire the necessary resources to eliminate or reduce the negative consequences of debt on your financial welfare.

"Categories of debt and their consequences."

Debt is a financial instrument that may have both advantageous and challenging implications, depending upon its management and use. Understanding the many forms of debt and its consequences is essential for people navigating their financial circumstances. Multiple varieties of debt exist, each with distinct attributes and outcomes for individual financial situations.

Consumer debt is the most prevalent, including credit card debts, personal loans, and other financial obligations acquired for every day costs or optional purchases. Although these loans provide rapid financial flexibility, they sometimes include high-interest rates, making them expensive if mishandled. Accruing consumer debt may result in financial stress and harm credit ratings, hindering one's ability to get advantageous interest rates in the future.

Mortgage debt is linked to real estate acquisition and is often considered a long-term investment. Although mortgages generally provide cheaper interest rates than consumer lending, they entail a substantial financial obligation. The consequences of mortgage debt include the gradual accumulation of home equity, the benefits of tax deductions via mortgage interest, and

the possibility of property value growth.

Nonetheless, the inability to fulfill mortgage responsibilities may lead to foreclosure and the forfeiture of the property.

Student loan debt is acquired for educational endeavors, and its consequences go beyond monetary issues. Education is a valuable investment for future income potential. However, having excessive student loan debt may be a long-term burden, impacting one's capacity to save, invest, and accomplish other financial objectives. Maintaining a harmonious equilibrium between allocating funds towards schooling and effectively handling student loan responsibilities is crucial for ensuring sustained financial well-being.

Auto loans are a financial obligation used to fund motor vehicle acquisition. Although a car loan offers instant mobility, it entails interest payments and the possibility of the vehicle's value decreasing over time. Failure to effectively handle vehicle loan responsibilities may lead to repossession, harming an individual's creditworthiness and overall financial stability.

Entrepreneurs or small company owners often accumulate business debt to finance operations, growth, or capital expenditures. Company debt, when properly managed, may stimulate development and enhance profitability. However, handling correctly can result in financial stability for the company owner. Gaining a comprehensive understanding of the consequences of corporate debt, such as the conditions for repayment and interest rates, is essential for ensuring the long-term viability of business operations.

To summarize, various forms of debt have specific consequences for people and corporations. Effectively managing debt requires a comprehensive grasp of the terms, interest rates, and possible implications on one's overall financial well-being. Achieving long-term financial success relies on effectively using debt for financial possibilities while avoiding excessive debt buildup.

"Techniques for prudent borrowing and the repayment of debt."

It is crucial to devise efficient tactics for responsible borrowing and debt settlement to maintain financial well-being and attain long-term financial objectives. Individuals may use many approaches to efficiently manage the intricacies of borrowing prudently and managing debt, whether they are contemplating acquiring new debt or resolving current commitments.

First and foremost, an essential element of prudent borrowing is completing a comprehensive evaluation of one's financial circumstances. This entails developing a comprehensive budget that delineates sources of income, expenditures, and objectives for saving. Through comprehending their financial capability, people may make well-informed choices about the level of debt they can prudently assume without jeopardizing their capacity to cover vital costs or invest in future necessities.

Selecting the appropriate kind of debt is an additional crucial tactic. Various forms of debt are associated with different interest rates, payback periods, and consequences. Lower-interest alternatives, such as secured loans or low-interest credit cards, may reduce borrowing expenses. Furthermore, it is crucial to consider the intended use of the debt; borrowing for investments that have the potential to provide profits, such as schooling or a house purchase, is more strategic than borrowing for non-essential expenses.

A thorough debt repayment strategy is crucial for effectively managing current financial responsibilities. People may strategically arrange their resources and effectively pay off their obligations by prioritizing loans with high-interest rates and using a structured technique like the debt avalanche or debt snowball method. Regular and punctual payments decrease the total expense of debt and aid in establishing a favorable credit record.

Negotiating with creditors is a proactive approach to effectively and reasonably managing debt. When confronted with financial difficulties, people should promptly contact their creditors to discuss their circumstances. Several creditors are open to negotiating alternate payment arrangements or providing temporary assistance, assisting debtors in avoiding default and possibly enduring repercussions on their credit ratings.

Ultimately, developing a mentality of fiscal restraint and embracing sustainable expenditure patterns is crucial for prudent borrowing and paying debts. This entails differentiating between necessities and non-essential desires, making deliberate financial decisions, and refraining from impulsive expenditures. Establishing an emergency fund may also function as a safeguard, offering a financial buffer to handle unforeseen costs without depending on further debt.

Appropriate borrowing and debt repayment need meticulous preparation, intelligent choices, and disciplined financial behaviors. By evaluating one's financial capability, selecting suitable forms of debt, devising a well-organized repayment strategy, engaging in negotiations with creditors as needed, and cultivating disciplined spending habits, individuals can effectively navigate the realm of borrowing and debt, thereby enhancing their financial expertise and ultimately striving towards a more stable and prosperous financial future.

"Developing a strategy to eradicate or control current debt."

Developing a thorough strategy to eradicate or control current debt is essential for financial stability and long-term prosperity. By carefully managing outstanding debts, people may alleviate financial strain, enhance creditworthiness, and lay the foundation for future financial prosperity. Below are essential measures to consider while formulating a debt removal strategy.

Initially, getting a comprehensive overview of the current outstanding bills is essential. Generate a comprehensive inventory including the debt category, remaining amount owed, interest rates, and minimum monthly payments. This inventory offers a comprehensive assessment of the whole debt load and serves as the basis for formulating a focused plan for repayment.

Ranking debts in importance is the subsequent vital phase in the planning procedure. Repaying high-interest debts, such as credit card bills, should be given priority because of the compounding effect of interest. The debt avalanche strategy directs additional cash towards the debt with the most significant interest rate while making just the minimum payments on the other debts. On the other hand, the debt snowball strategy prioritizes the repayment of the lowest debts first, resulting in psychological victories and increased motivation with each cleared obligation.

Creating a budget is a crucial element of any strategy to eliminate debt. A budget enables people to arrange their income towards necessary expenditures, debt settlement, and savings. Individuals may expedite decreasing outstanding amounts by identifying areas for expenditure reduction and allocating surplus income toward debt repayment.

Engaging in negotiations with creditors is a proactive approach worth considering. Communication with creditors to explore the potential for reducing interest rates, modifying payment arrangements, or negotiating settlements may provide respite and facilitate repaying debts. Several creditors are willing to examine mutually advantageous resolutions, particularly if they increase their chances of receiving payments.

Consistency and discipline are crucial for successfully implementing a debt removal strategy. Implementing a consistent schedule for making periodic payments, either monthly or bi-weekly, is essential for sustaining momentum and guaranteeing advancement toward achieving a debt-free status. Maintaining unwavering dedication to the strategy, especially when facing unforeseen expenditures or financial obstacles, is crucial for enduring success.

To summarize, developing a strategy to eradicate or handle current debt requires a systematic and tactical approach. People may take many steps to gain control over their financial destiny and strive for a life free of debt. These include evaluating all outstanding debts, determining repayment priorities, establishing a budget, negotiating with creditors, and sustaining consistent efforts. This procedure alleviates current monetary pressures and establishes the foundation for enhanced fiscal stability and the achievement of forthcoming financial objectives.

Chapter 8

Building and Protecting Credit

Credit is a fundamental aspect of financial stability, and Chapter 8 provides detailed instructions on establishing and maintaining a favorable credit history. Acquire the skills to navigate the credit environment effectively via astute decision-making and avoid typical traps.

"Recognizing the significance of a favorable credit score."

Comprehending the significance of a strong credit score is essential for effectively managing one's financial health and obtaining advantageous borrowing conditions. A credit score is a quantitative measure of an individual's ability to repay debts, playing a vital role for lenders, landlords, and employers in assessing financial reliability. The importance of keeping a high credit score cannot be exaggerated since it impacts all facets of an individual's financial well-being.

First and foremost, a high credit score significantly influences the ability to get advantageous interest rates for loans and credit cards. Lenders use credit scores to evaluate the likelihood of granting a loan to a person. A better credit score indicates prudent financial conduct, resulting in reduced interest rates and the possibility of significant savings during the loan's duration. This advantage applies to various credit options, such as mortgages, vehicles, and personal loans.

Furthermore, a favorable credit score is essential for accessing broader financial prospects. Individuals with elevated credit scores have a greater probability of obtaining approval for credit cards that provide enticing rewards programs, increased credit limits, and more favorable conditions. Moreover, a strong credit history increases the probability of being approved for rental applications. It potentially influences career chances since some firms consider credit scores when hiring.

Moreover, a favorable credit score is crucial in establishing a robust financial base. A solid credit history indicates prudent financial management, including punctual payments and keeping minimal credit card balances. Consequently, this improves an individual's total financial standing, thus establishing credibility with financial institutions and other interested parties.

Furthermore, a commendable credit score might enhance insurance costs and aid loan accessibility. Several insurance firms use credit information to evaluate the likelihood of providing insurance coverage to a person. Individuals with elevated credit scores may be eligible for reduced insurance rates, regardless of whether it is for automobile, homeowners, or renters' insurance. This exemplifies the extensive influence of credit ratings on all facets of personal finance.

Finally, a high credit score is crucial for successfully managing life changes. A solid credit history facilitates significant life choices such as purchasing a house, funding a school, or establishing a company. A robust credit score provides people the capacity and advantage to pursue their objectives and ambitions actively, thus enhancing their financial autonomy and stability.

Ultimately, comprehending the significance of a commendable credit score is crucial for individuals aiming to make well-informed financial choices and get advantageous conditions in different areas of life. A strong credit history provides access to improved borrowing options, financial flexibility, and overall well-being. Through proactive management and prioritization of credit health, people may strategically position themselves for success in their financial pursuits.

"Strategies for establishing and maintaining a favorable credit record."

Establishing and sustaining a solid credit record is crucial for obtaining advantageous financial prospects and guaranteeing sustained financial stability. A favorable credit history showcases prudent financial conduct and improves an individual's creditworthiness, granting access to more favorable interest rates, loan approvals, and other financial benefits. Below are some guidelines for establishing and maintaining a favorable credit record.

First and foremost, properly build credit. If you are inexperienced with credit, it is advisable to begin by obtaining a secured credit card, becoming an authorized user on another individual's account, consistently making payments on time, and using credit responsibly from the start to help establish a favorable credit history. For those with a well-established credit history, it is advisable to maintain responsible credit use by ensuring timely payment of bills and refraining from accumulating excessive debt.

Ensuring regular and punctual payments is crucial for establishing and maintaining a favorable credit record. The payment history plays a vital role in the computation of credit ratings, and even a solitary delayed payment might result in an adverse effect.

Establish automated payments or notifications to guarantee timely payment of bills. Punctual payments add to a favorable credit history and build a consistent pattern of prudent financial conduct.

Ensure a minimal credit-use ratio. This ratio represents the proportion of used credit from the total available credit. A lower credit usage ratio is often advantageous and may influence credit ratings. To exhibit prudent credit management, maintain credit card balances much lower than the credit limit, preferably below 30%.

Consistently monitor credit reports to ensure accuracy and swiftly resolve any inconsistencies. Acquire complimentary yearly credit reports from all major credit agencies and scrutinize them for inaccuracies or deceitful actions. Challenging mistakes and swiftly resolving concerns might prevent them from negatively impacting credit ratings. Several credit monitoring services provide continuous access to credit records and ratings.

Ultimately, exercise careful planning when it comes to terminating accounts. Shutting down credit accounts may affect the duration of one's credit history and the percentage of credit being used. When contemplating the closure of an account, carefully assess the possible consequences on the comprehensive credit profile. Maintaining an older account and utilizing it appropriately might have a beneficial impact on one's credit history.

Establishing and maintaining a favorable credit record requires prudent credit use, regular, punctual payments, and diligent oversight. Individuals can cultivate a favorable credit history and enhance their long-term financial success by responsibly establishing credit, ensuring timely payments, effectively managing credit utilization, regularly monitoring credit reports for accuracy, and strategically considering account closures.

"Preventing typical errors that might negatively impact credit."

It is essential to be mindful of typical mistakes that might negatively impact one's credit, which is vital for maintaining a favorable credit record and overall financial stability. Establishing credit is crucial, but specific errors may have enduring repercussions on credit scores and overall trustworthiness. Here are some essential guidelines to avoid frequent mistakes that might negatively impact credit.

Consistently making late payments is a very damaging conduct that may significantly damage one's credit. The payment history has excellent importance in credit scoring models, and even a solitary instance of late payment may lead to a discernible decrease in credit ratings. Implement reminders, automate payments, or build a budgeting system to guarantee timely payment of bills.

Exceeding the credit limit on credit cards and maintaining substantial outstanding debts are other prevalent mistakes that may negatively impact one's credit score. Credit ratings are significantly affected by the credit usage ratio, representing the proportion of available credit currently being used. Maintaining credit card balances much lower than the credit limit, preferably around 30%, showcases prudent credit management and positively affects credit ratings.

Shutting down previous credit accounts may also harm credit ratings since it reduces the total duration of credit history. The duration of credit history is a significant determinant of credit scores, and terminating accounts that have been open for a long time might hurt this element. Retaining existing accounts and using them appropriately to maintain a lengthier credit history is advisable.

Engaging in many applications for new credit accounts within a short timeframe, sometimes called a "credit shopping spree," may harm credit ratings. Whenever an application is submitted, it generates a hard inquiry on the credit report. If several inquiries are made quickly, it indicates financial difficulty.

Exercise prudence while pursuing credit and only pursue additional accounts when needed.

Neglecting credit reports and neglecting to check for inaccuracies or fraudulent behavior is a prevalent mistake that may result in significant repercussions. Monitor credit reports for discrepancies or questionable activities and swiftly challenge any errors. Prompt detection and settlement of problems may avert their adverse effects on credit scores.

To summarize, preventing frequent mistakes that negatively impact credit requires a proactive and disciplined strategy toward credit management. Individuals may safeguard and maintain their credit health by continually ensuring timely payments, maintaining a low credit use ratio, retaining existing accounts, strategically managing new credit applications, and routinely reviewing credit reports. These acts facilitate the establishment of a favorable credit record, granting access to improved financial prospects and ensuring sustained financial stability in the long run.

Chapter 9

Navigating Career and Income

Chapter 9 provides a comprehensive examination of financial well-being by investigating the point where professional choices, income, and financial planning converge. Explore the essential factors for achieving a rewarding and economically viable profession, including salary negotiation and balancing passion and pragmatism.

"The correlation between career choices, earnings, and economic prosperity."

The correlation between profession selection, earnings, and financial stability is crucial to an individual's financial situation. Career choices have a vital influence on the amount of money one may make, which substantially affects one's financial well. The link among these variables is complex and diverse, impacting several facets of an individual's financial life.

The profession one chooses primarily establishes the foundation for one's prospective earnings. Various occupations and sectors provide different remuneration systems and opportunities for income generation. Technology, finance, or healthcare professions can provide more excellent salary prospects than specific service or entry-level roles. Engaging in well-informed and strategic decision-making about one's profession, taking into account personal interests, abilities, and market demand, has the potential to result in increased earning capacity and financial security.

The financial well-being of an individual is directly impacted by the revenue earned from their chosen profession. An increased income allows people to cover necessary living costs, accumulate savings for the future, and experience a certain level of comfort and quality of life. It provides financial adaptability and the capacity to withstand unforeseen costs or economic downturns. Conversely, a reduced income may need meticulous budgeting and strategic financial planning to guarantee economic stability and achieve long-term objectives.

Furthermore, the correlation between professional decisions and financial prosperity goes beyond the mere amount of money made. Some professions may provide extra financial perks, such as employer-funded pension schemes, medical coverage, or performance-based incentives. These benefits enhance overall financial stability and influence an individual's capacity to save for retirement, handle healthcare expenses, and meet other financial obligations.

Their career choices also impact one's financial path over time. Progressions, elevations, and prospects for professional development may result in augmented earnings and enhanced financial prosperity. On the other hand, if a person's chosen job is not progressing or seeing restricted growth, they may need to seek other opportunities to gain new skills or consider other career routes to improve their ability to generate money and increase their financial prospects.

Ultimately, the correlation between professional decisions, earnings, and overall financial stability is vital to individual financial management. Making well-informed choices about one's professional trajectory establishes the basis for earning capacity and financial security. It influences day-to-day financial decisions, strategic planning, and the capacity to accomplish financial objectives. By carefully aligning their employment choices with their financial ambitions, people may optimize their income, boost their financial well-being, and strive toward a more stable and prosperous future.

"Discuss appropriate compensation, perks, and strategic financial management for professional advancement."

Engaging in discussions about wages, benefits, and financial planning is crucial for advancing one's career, enabling people to optimize their compensation packages and proactively prepare for their financial well-being. Salary negotiation is fighting for equitable remuneration corresponding to one's expertise, background, and the worth one provides to a company. Effective bargaining improves one's financial situation and establishes a foundation for future income and professional advancement.

Benefits negotiation is an essential component of complete pay packages. In addition to income, negotiating benefits such as healthcare, retirement plans, and other perks may substantially influence an individual's financial situation. Assessing the worth of benefits, bargaining for more excellent coverage, or pursuing extra advantages such as flexible work arrangements may lead to increased financial stability and a better equilibrium between work and personal life.

Financial planning is vital to advancing one's profession, including establishing immediate and future objectives. Engaging in wage and benefits negotiations allows individuals to carefully prepare for critical financial goals, such as purchasing a house, saving for college, or establishing a retirement fund. A thorough financial plan includes carefully allocating funds, setting aside only for future use, making strategic investments, and practical and aging debt. This ensures t

Advancements in one's profession directly contribute to achieving specific financial goals.

Furthermore, the ability to negotiate is not limited to receiving job offers but may be used in all aspects of one's professional journey. Engaging in regular evaluations and discussions on pay and benefits, whether at performance evaluations or when assuming more duties, demonstrates proactive career management. The continuing negotiation cultivates a mutually advantageous connection with employers, showcasing an individual's dedication to constant development and value generation.

To summarize, the crucial aspects of advancing one's career include engaging in pay negotiations, discussing benefits, and participating in strategic financial planning. These abilities enable people to champion equitable remuneration, maximize perks packages, and effectively prepare for their financial prospects. By using skillful bargaining techniques and careful financial strategizing, people may improve their current financial situation and establish a strategic plan for continuous professional advancement and enduring financial prosperity.

"Achieving a harmonious equilibrium between one's hunger and pragmatism while making professional choices."

Striking a balance between enthusiasm and pragmatism in job choices is a sensitive but essential endeavor people encounter while navigating their professional trajectories. On one side, choosing a profession that aligns with one's interests may result in a gratifying and meaningful professional existence. Conversely, pragmatic factors, such as economic stability and employment market requirements, often substantially influence guaranteeing a stable and enduring profession. A harmonious equilibrium between these elements is crucial for achieving personal contentment and occupational prosperity.

Passion ignites enthusiasm and commitment, propelling people to flourish in their chosen domains. When a profession is in harmony with one's interests and desires, employment transcends being a simple occupation. It evolves into a gratifying calling that elicits happiness and a profound feeling of meaning. This inherent incentive may increase work satisfaction, inventiveness, and the ability to bounce back from difficulties. Careers fueled by passion often lead to profoundly involved and dedicated people, contributing to personal development and satisfaction.

Nevertheless, it is crucial to recognize the pragmatic elements of professional choices. Market demand, wage potential, and employment stability guarantee financial stability and long-term sustainability. Finding a middle ground between following one's passion and making pragmatic decisions that align with the current labor market trends and economic circumstances is necessary. Adopting this practical approach is crucial for establishing a long-lasting profession that can withstand economic volatility and provide a secure basis for personal and financial development.

A balance between passion and pragmatism requires deliberate self-reflection and thorough investigation. Individuals can assess how their passions correspond with the requirements of the work market and pinpoint areas where they may use their talents and interests to have the most influence. This may include identifying sectors or positions that combine personal satisfaction and pragmatism, enabling people to excel in their professions while achieving financial and professional objectives.

Furthermore, a dynamic and ever-changing job market often enables individuals to incorporate their passions into various positions and sectors. Instead of seeing passion and pragmatism as incompatible, people might discover methods to integrate their interests into many facets of their professional lives. This strategy allows individuals to engage in meaningful employment while prioritizing practicalities to assure stability and advancement.

To summarize, achieving a balance between passion and pragmatism while making job selections is a complex task that demands thoughtful contemplation and introspection. People may construct gratifying, enduring, and adaptable professions by harmonizing one's interests with pragmatic concerns. The crucial factor is discovering a harmonic amalgamation that permits individual contentment and vocational accomplishment, resulting in a gratifying and well-rounded professional trajectory.

Chapter 10

Long-Term Wealth and Future Planning

As we approach the end of our trip, Chapter 10 encourages you to reflect on the long-term implications. Delve into the complexities of retirement and estate planning, establishing a foundation for a future that is both financially stable and in harmony with your greatest desires. This chapter provides a clear plan for creating a lasting impact beyond the current moment.

"Mindful Money Mastery" aims to provide you with the information, skills, and mentality needed to manage your finances effectively. It helps you make financial decisions that align with your values and contribute to a future of prosperity and satisfaction while adapting to the ever-changing financial environment.

"Financial strategizing for individuals in the early stages of their careers to prepare for retirement."

Planning for retirement at a young age is an essential financial task frequently neglected due to the urgent responsibilities of early adulthood. Commencing retirement planning at an early stage offers a notable benefit, enabling people to use the potential of compounding and establish a solid financial base for their future years. Below are essential factors for young folks beginning their retirement planning endeavor.

First and foremost, understanding the notion of compounding is of utmost importance. Young individuals may capitalize on the compounding impact by initiating retirement savings and investments at an early stage. This effect allows investment profits to create supplementary returns as time progresses. The compounding process may significantly increase the money saved for retirement, highlighting the need to contribute to retirement accounts as early as feasible.

Comprehending and using employer-provided retirement plans, such as 401(k)s or RRSPs in Canada, is another crucial component of retirement planning for young individuals. Several businesses have retirement savings programs that include matching payments, which may accelerate the growth of retirement funds. Young individuals should strive to contribute a sufficient amount to take full advantage of the employer match, maximizing the benefits of this crucial working perk.

Ensuring a diverse range of assets within retirement accounts is essential for effectively controlling risk and maximizing returns. Young folks often have more time to invest, enabling them to endure market changes and take advantage of investment opportunities that carry more risk and provide more significant potential returns. An extensively diversified portfolio, including a combination of equities, fixed-income securities, and many other assets, effectively reduces risk and corresponds with long-term retirement objectives.

Young individuals may create a significant retirement fund by making regular and increasing payments over time. Consistently contributing to retirement accounts, even with small amounts, develops a routine of saving and investing. As one's salary increases during one's career, one can steadily raise one's contributions, taking advantage of continuous saving and higher earning capacity.

Lastly, it is essential to be well-informed and regularly reevaluate retirement plans as financial objectives and circumstances change. It is advisable for young individuals to periodically evaluate their retirement accounts, analyze their investing strategy, and modify contributions in response to changing financial circumstances. This proactive strategy guarantees that retirement plans stay aligned with individual objectives and any changes in economic circumstances.

Ultimately, retirement planning in young people's financial strategy is crucial for achieving sustained financial prosperity. Young individuals may establish a solid foundation for a safe and satisfying retirement by using the benefits of compounding, optimizing employer-sponsored retirement plans, diversifying assets, maintaining regular contributions, and being well-informed. By taking these proactive measures early in their careers, young individuals can strengthen their financial prospects and confidently attain their retirement objectives.

"The significance of estate planning and the need to establish a will."

Estate planning is an essential and sometimes disregarded component of financial administration, centered on establishing a will. A will is a legally binding document specifying the management of an individual's assets and affairs upon death. Although estate planning is significant, many individuals, particularly young ones, may fail to see its pressing need. Nevertheless, drafting a will is a conscientious and proactive choice with substantial consequences for the beneficiaries and the allocation of an individual's possessions.

The main objective of a will is to provide explicit directives for allocating an individual's wealth among designated beneficiaries. Without a will, the distribution of assets is determined by state laws, often called intestacy laws. This might result in results that may not correspond to the desires of the dead individual. Drafting a will guarantees that an individual's possessions are distributed to the desired recipients, including family members, acquaintances, or philanthropic institutions.

Furthermore, a will enables people to choose an executor who will oversee the administration of the estate and execute the directives specified in the will. The executor is responsible for managing the legal and financial matters of the dead individual, which includes resolving outstanding debts, allocating assets, and navigating through any legal procedures.

A will is crucial for families with underage children since it allows them to choose guardianship. In the absence of explicit guidance, the courts may be required to determine the guardianship of underage children in the case of their parent's death. Using a testament, people may choose a guardian of their choice, guaranteeing that their children are looked after by someone they have confidence in and who upholds their principles.

A will is a dynamic document that may be revised to reflect changing circumstances. Life events such as weddings, divorces, babies, or changes in financial position may need modifications to the will. Consistently examining and revising the will guarantees that it accurately reflects an individual's desires and circumstances.

To summarize, drafting a will is a fundamental aspect of efficient estate planning, allowing people to specify the allocation of their assets, choose reliable executors, and assign guardians for underage children. Although reflecting on one's mortality may be unsettling, creating a will is a pragmatic and empathetic approach to guaranteeing the well-being of loved ones and adequately administrating one's estate according to their desires. People actively enhance the financial stability and emotional tranquility of themselves and their families by allocating the necessary time to draft a will.

"Establishing a durable and satisfying financial future."

Establishing a sustainable and gratifying financial future is a comprehensive undertaking beyond acquiring ring riches. It encompasses a holistic approach to achieving financial stability by including individual values, future objectives, and wise financial strategies. The core of this path is developing financial resilience and a mentality that effectively balances immediate demands with long-term goals.

To begin this journey, it is essential to establish unambiguous financial objectives. These objectives serve as guiding lights, directing your financial choices and activities. By clearly defining precise and attainable goals, such as purchasing a house, financing college, or achieving a comfortable retirement, you may customize your financial plan to align with these objectives.

Establishing and maintaining a budget is a fundamental aspect of successful financial management. A well-designed budget guarantees that your expenses are by your aims and enables you to save and invest with discipline. Monitoring expenditures allows you to identify opportunities for possible cost reductions, allocating more resources toward attaining your financial objectives.

Long-term investment is a crucial aspect of establishing a financially secure future. It is advisable to spread your assets over many asset categories to reduce risk and avoid the need to pursue immediate profits. Adhering to a regular and controlled investment strategy and comprehending the potency of compounding may significantly enhance wealth building over an extended period.

Prudently handling debt is a crucial component of maintaining long-term financial stability. Although some debts, like mortgages, might serve as strategic investments, consumer debt with high-interest rates can impede financial advancement. Create a systematic strategy to repay high-interest loans, allocating more resources towards wealth accumulation and alleviating financial strain.

It is crucial to prioritize acquiring financial knowledge and engaging in ongoing learning. Keeping up to date with investing techniques, tax consequences, and economic trends enables you to make well-informed choices in the ever-changing financial environment. Frequently evaluate your financial plan, making necessary modifications to suit changes in living circumstances, professional transitions, and growing goals.

Constructing a sustainable and satisfying financial future requires a comprehensive and purposeful strategy. By establishing explicit objectives, maintaining a strict financial plan, making prudent investments, strategically handling debt, and consistently expanding your knowledge, you can not only amass wealth but also cultivate a state of financial prosperity that harmonizes with your principles and brings satisfaction to different facets of your life.

Conclusion

As we wrap up our investigation into "Mindful Money Mastery: Navigating the Psychology of Finance in Your 20s," I hope this expedition has been enlightening and inspiring. The chapters have explored the complicated interplay between your thoughts, emotions, and financial choices, providing valuable insights and ways to navigate the intricacies of personal finance during this transitional period.

In one's twenties, individuals embark on self-exploration, personal development, and establishing the groundwork for their future endeavors. The ideas elucidated in this book pertain to financial management and the cultivation of awareness, the deliberate selection of options, and the harmonization of financial decisions with one's ambitions.

The preceding pages examined the importance of comprehending your attitude toward money, establishing conscientious financial objectives, managing the emotional factors that impact spending, and accepting the fundamental investing principles. We have explored the cognitive biases that influence your financial decision-making and techniques for effectively handling debt. We have explored the correlation between your professional decisions, earnings, and financial welfare.

While contemplating the knowledge acquired, it is essential to acknowledge that this is not your financial expedition's conclusion but a significant stride towards conscientiously managing your finances. To effectively use these concepts, it is crucial to customize them according to your circumstances, objectives, and aspirations. Your financial future is constantly changing, and you have the power to mold it.

Please continue to adhere to the principles of mindful money management as you make financial choices that align with your beliefs and goals. May your twenties catalyze a prosperous future with financial stability, personal satisfaction, and achieving your aspirations. May you achieve a financially secure and robust future in your twenties and beyond by being attentive to your financial decisions.

We appreciate your participation in our endeavor. May your financial journey be abundant with conscientious choices, deliberate decisions, and attaining your most treasured objectives.

Acknowledgments

Authoring a book is an expedition, and I profoundly appreciate the people who contributed to the genesis of "Mindful Money Mastery: Navigating the Psychology of Finance in Your 20s." Their assistance, direction, and motivation were crucial in completing this project.

I sincerely appreciate the following:

My Family's steadfast support, encouragement, and understanding during the several hours dedicated to studying and writing.

My Friends: I am grateful for their inspiration, valuable ideas, and support throughout the difficult moments of my writing path.

Mentors and advisors: Their sagacity and counsel enhanced the substance of this book, molding it into a complete and thoughtful manual for young people navigating the intricacies of personal finance.

Individuals who engage in reading: The individual's curiosity and desire for knowledge inspired me to investigate further the subjects discussed in this book. We value your involvement and input.

Bibliography

The following resources have been instrumental in shaping the content of "Mindful Money Mastery." I am indebted to the authors, researchers, and educators whose work has enriched the insights shared in this book.

Brown, B. (2010). "The Gifts of Imperfection: Let Go of Who You Think You're Supposed to Be and Embrace Who You Are." Hazelden Publishing.

Duhigg, C. (2012). "The Power of Habit: Why We Do What We Do in Life and Business." Random House.

Kobliner, B. (2017). "Get a Financial Life: Personal Finance in Your Twenties and Thirties." Simon & Schuster.

Thaler, R. H., & Sunstein, C. R. (2008). "Nudge: Improving Decisions About Health, Wealth, and Happiness." Penguin Books.

Lusardi, A., & Mitchell, O. S. (2007). "Baby Boomer Retirement Security: The Roles of Planning, Financial Literacy, and Housing Wealth." Journal of Monetary Economics, 54(1), 205–224.

Vanguard. (2019). "How America Invests 2019: A Report on Vanguard Retail Investor Activity." Vanguard Group.

These resources represent a fraction of the wealth of knowledge available, and I encourage readers to explore further and continue their journey toward financial mastery and mindfulness.

Disclaimer

The content in the book "Mindful Money Mastery: Navigating the Psychology of Finance in Your 20s" is meant to serve as general information and should not be considered financial, investing, or professional advice. The author needs the credentials of a certified financial counselor, and the information presented in this book should not be regarded as a replacement for personalized financial advice from a professional.

The content of this book may need to be updated due to the dynamic nature of financial markets and laws. The author does not provide any guarantees or assurances, whether explicit or implicit, about the comprehensiveness, correctness, dependability, appropriateness, or accessibility of the information, goods, services, or associated visuals included in this book. Consequently, whatever trust you put in this material is entirely your responsibility.

Readers should get guidance from a certified financial counselor, accountant, or legal expert before making any financial choices. The author and publisher absolve themselves of all responsibility for any loss or harm, including but not limited to indirect or consequential loss or damage, resulting from the reliance on the information provided in this book.

The author's inclusion of links or references to third-party websites, goods, or services should not be interpreted as an endorsement or suggestion. The author bears no responsibility for other websites' information, accuracy, or practices.

Readers should use their discernment in implementing the principles and tactics elucidated in this book to their financial circumstances. Individual financial situations vary, and what may be suitable for one individual may not be ideal for another. The author encourages readers to conduct thorough research and seek professional advice tailored to their needs before implementing financial strategies.

By reading this book, you acknowledge and agree to the terms of this disclaimer.

Insight Secret Collection

www.ingramcontent.com/pod-product-compliance
Lightning Source LLC
Chambersburg PA
CBHW071055290526
45795CB00004B/1496